THANKSGIVING
DAY
CRAFTS

by Jean Eick

Library of Congress Cataloging-in-Publication Data
Eick, Jean. 1947-
Thanksgiving Crafts / by Jean Eick.
p. cm.
Includes index.
Summary: Includes lists of things needed and specific directions
for making a variety of crafts related to Thanksgiving.
ISBN 1-56766-534-9 (library bound : alk. paper)

1. Thanksgiving decorations — Juvenile literature.
2. Handicraft — Juvenile literature.
[1. Thanksgiving decorations. 2. Handicraft.]
I. Title.

TT900.T6E95 1998	98-13109
745.594'1 — dc21	CIP
	AC

GRAPHIC DESIGN & ILLUSTRATION
Robert A. Honey, Seattle

PRODUCTION COORDINATION
James R. Rothaus / James R. Rothaus & Associates

ELECTRONIC PRE-PRESS PRODUCTION
Robert E. Bonaker / Graphic Design & Consulting Company

CONTENTS

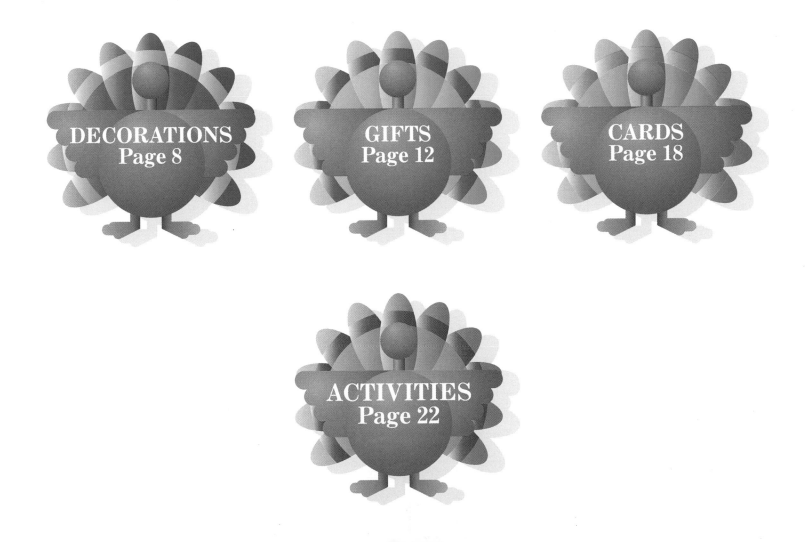

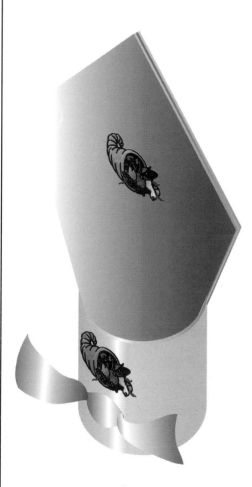

1 Thanksgiving is a very special day. It's a time for people to be thankful for the things they have. It's also a day to remember the early settlers of the United States. Making crafts is one special way you can share in this holiday. This book will show you how to make some fun Thanksgiving crafts to give and enjoy.

2 Before you start making any craft, be sure to read the directions. Make sure you look at the pictures too, they will help you understand what to do. Go through the list of things you'll need and get everything together. When you're ready, find a good place to work. Now you can begin making your crafts!

These turkeys look nice on windows and walls.

HAND PRINT TURKEY

Scissors.

Brown Construction Paper.

Crayons.

Markers.

Pencil.

1 Put your hand on a brown piece of paper. Make sure you stick your thumb out, just like the picture shows. Now draw around your hand.

2 Carefully cut out the shape.

3 Color the fingers to look like feathers.

4

Draw the turkey's eyes. Presto, a turkey!

A turkey is not just to eat on Thanksgiving. This turkey is to be made and admired.

PAPER BAG TURKEY

Scissors.

One Brown Pipe Cleaner.

A Brown Paper Lunch Bag.

News Paper

A Small White Paper Plate.

Tape.

A Rubber Band.

Colored Markers Or Crayons.

1 Fill the lunch bag with crumpled newspaper. Leave a little room at the top.

2 Put the rubber band around the top to keep the newspaper inside.

3 Crunch the bag together to make the turkey's body.

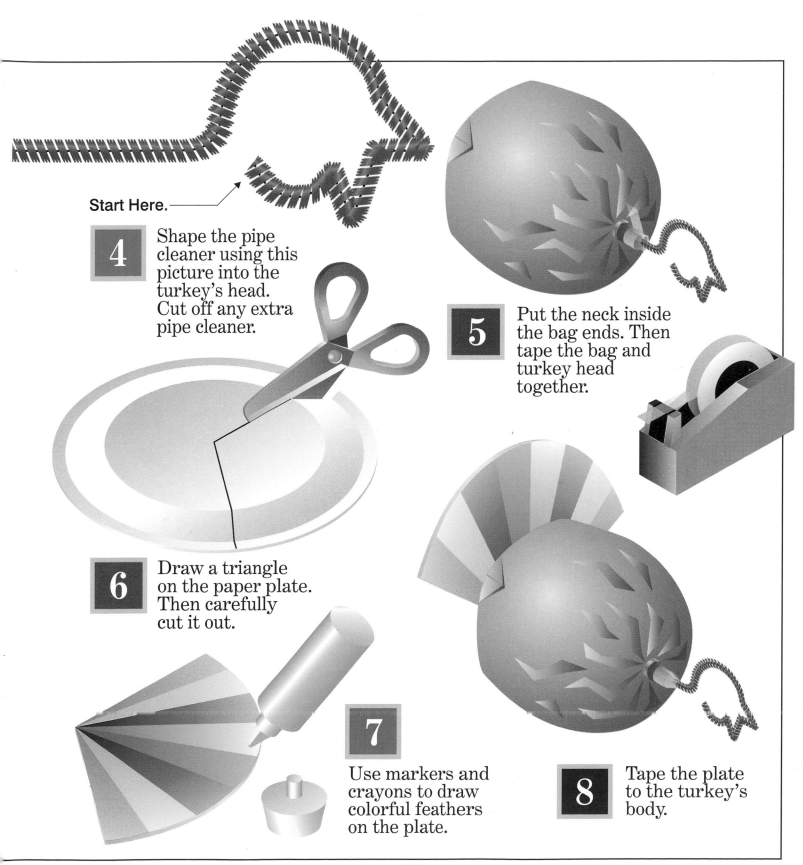

Start Here.

4 Shape the pipe cleaner using this picture into the turkey's head. Cut off any extra pipe cleaner.

5 Put the neck inside the bag ends. Then tape the bag and turkey head together.

6 Draw a triangle on the paper plate. Then carefully cut it out.

7 Use markers and crayons to draw colorful feathers on the plate.

8 Tape the plate to the turkey's body.

*Make lots of napkins.
Give some away and
save some for your
Thanksgiving dinner!*

DECORATED NAPKINS

Things You'll Need

*Plain Paper Napkins
From The
Grocery
Store.*

Things for Decorating

Crayons.

Markers.

*Stickers
Are Great.*

1 Fold the napkins the way you want them to look on the table. You can fold them in half or even make a triangle.

2 Decorate just the front of each napkin. You can make them all different or make them all the same.

Instead of napkin rings that fit around the middle of your napkins, these nice holders stand up the napkins.

NAPKIN HOLDERS

Things You'll Need

Scissors.

Poster Board.

Pencil.

Ribbon.

Ruler.

Hole Puncher.

Stapler.

1 Draw a rectangle that is 3 inches wide and 8 inches long on the poster board.

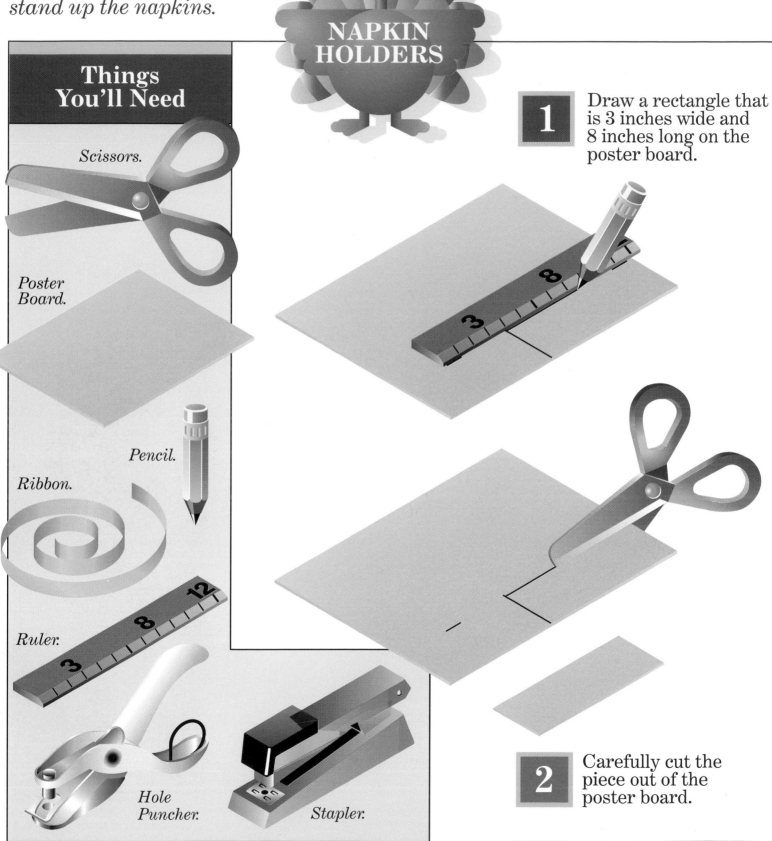

2 Carefully cut the piece out of the poster board.

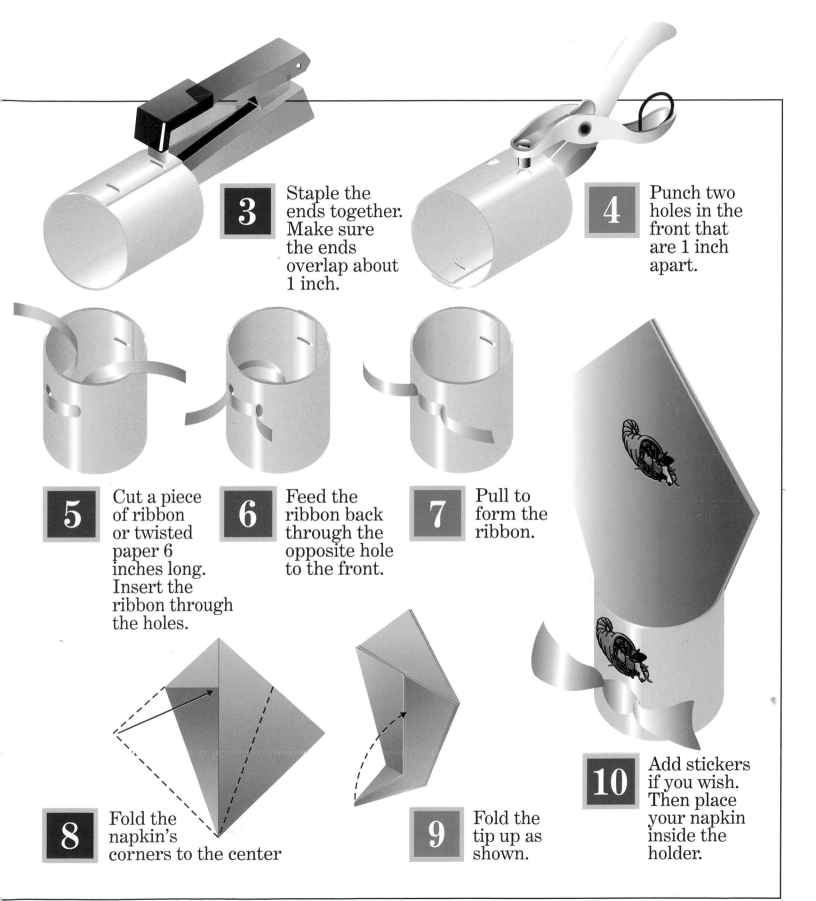

3 Staple the ends together. Make sure the ends overlap about 1 inch.

4 Punch two holes in the front that are 1 inch apart.

5 Cut a piece of ribbon or twisted paper 6 inches long. Insert the ribbon through the holes.

6 Feed the ribbon back through the opposite hole to the front.

7 Pull to form the ribbon.

8 Fold the napkin's corners to the center

9 Fold the tip up as shown.

10 Add stickers if you wish. Then place your napkin inside the holder.

This gift will make someone's Thanksgiving dinner table very special.

TABLE RUNNER

Things You'll Need

Scissors.

1 Roll Of Brown Mailing Paper.

Things for Decorating

Crayons.

Stickers

Markers.

Leaves Are Great.

 1 Roll out enough paper to cover the middle of the table. Then cut it off. Be sure to leave enough on each end to hang down a little.

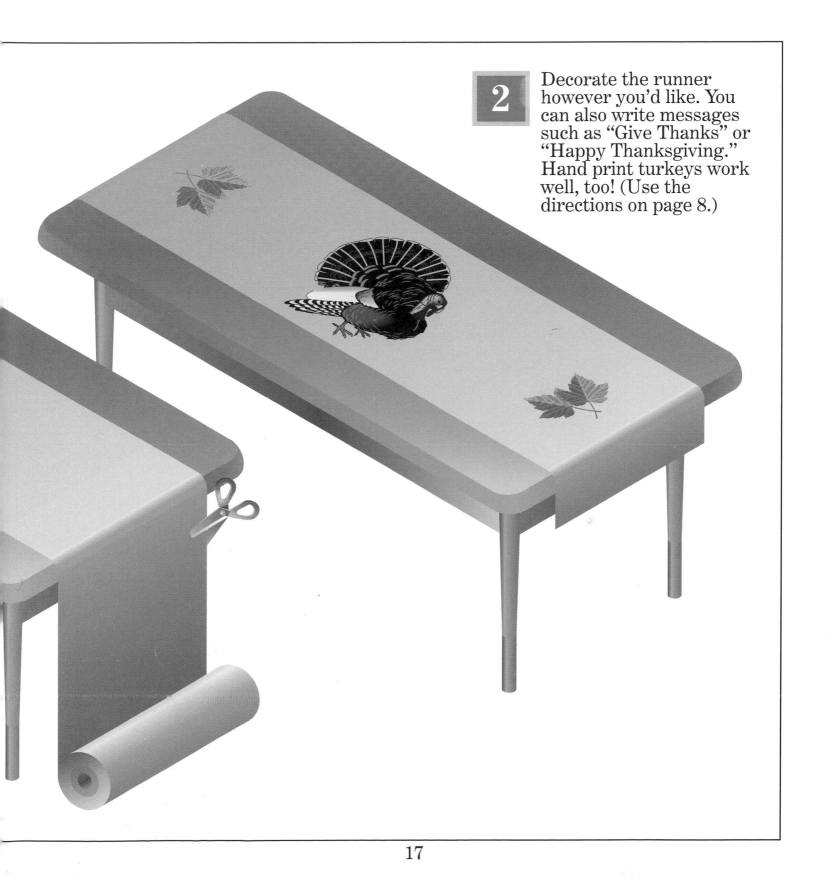

2 Decorate the runner however you'd like. You can also write messages such as "Give Thanks" or "Happy Thanksgiving." Hand print turkeys work well, too! (Use the directions on page 8.)

Thanksgiving cards are nice to give to your grandparents, parents, teachers, or friends.

CARDS

Things You'll Need

Scissors.

Crayons, Markers, or Paints. *Pencil.* *Glue.*

Construction Paper.

1 Fold the paper to the size you want your card to be. Folding it once will make a large card.

2 Folding it twice will make a small card.

3 Decorate the front of the card.

4 Write a message on the inside of the card. You can decorate the inside, too. Don't forget to sign your name.

Things for Decorating

Ribbon.

Buttons.

Glitter.

Stickers Are Great.

Here are some ideas for making your cards even more special!

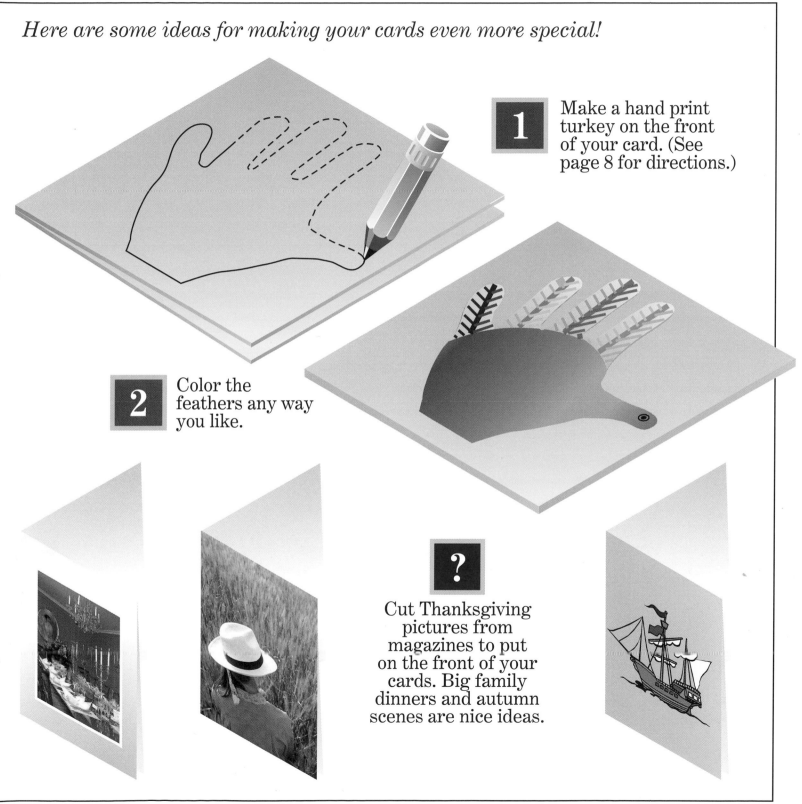

1 Make a hand print turkey on the front of your card. (See page 8 for directions.)

2 Color the feathers any way you like.

? Cut Thanksgiving pictures from magazines to put on the front of your cards. Big family dinners and autumn scenes are nice ideas.

You can even make your own envelopes to fit your cards!

ENVELOPES

Things You'll Need

Scissors.

Construction Paper, Wrapping Paper, or Paper Bag.

Pencil.

Tape or Glue.

Ruler.

To make a square envelope:

1 Cut out the front of a plain paper bag. It will take an 8 inch square piece of paper to hold a 5¼ inch square card.

2 Cut out a square 8 inches high and 8 inches across. Measure and put an "X" in the center of the square.

3 Fold three of the corners so they cover the "X". Tape or glue the corners so they'll stay in place.

4 Place your card inside, then fold the top down and tape it shut.

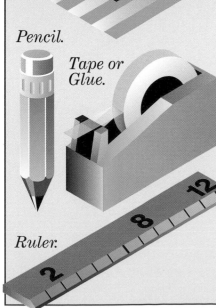

20

To make an envelope that isn't square:

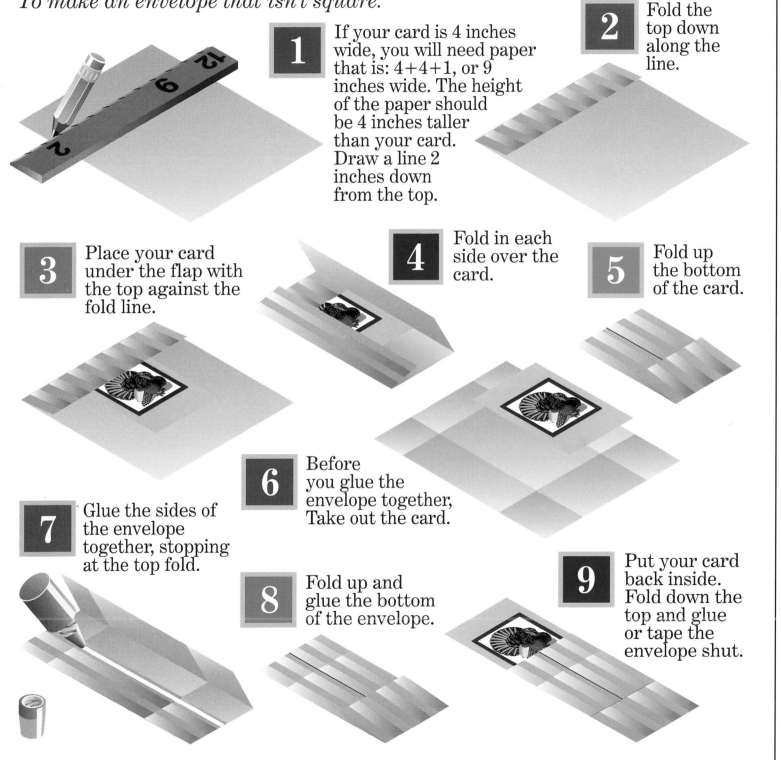

1 If your card is 4 inches wide, you will need paper that is: 4+4+1, or 9 inches wide. The height of the paper should be 4 inches taller than your card. Draw a line 2 inches down from the top.

2 Fold the top down along the line.

3 Place your card under the flap with the top against the fold line.

4 Fold in each side over the card.

5 Fold up the bottom of the card.

6 Before you glue the envelope together, Take out the card.

7 Glue the sides of the envelope together, stopping at the top fold.

8 Fold up and glue the bottom of the envelope.

9 Put your card back inside. Fold down the top and glue or tape the envelope shut.

There are many things you can do with others to celebrate Thanksgiving. Here are some fun ideas.

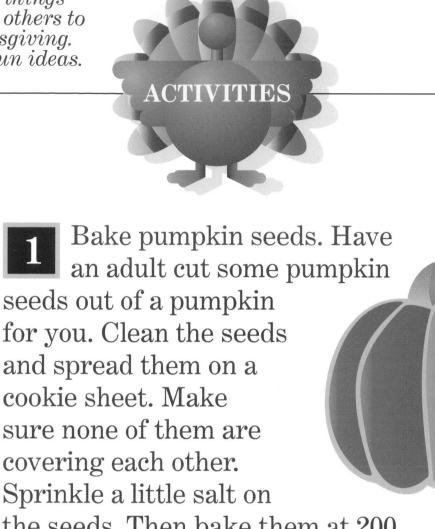

ACTIVITIES

1 Bake pumpkin seeds. Have an adult cut some pumpkin seeds out of a pumpkin for you. Clean the seeds and spread them on a cookie sheet. Make sure none of them are covering each other. Sprinkle a little salt on the seeds. Then bake them at 200 degrees until they are very dry and hard.

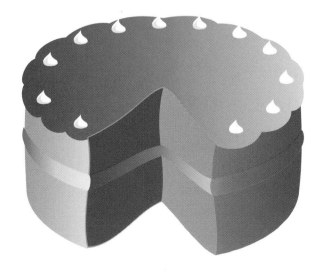

2 Help an adult make one of the dishes for Thanksgiving dinner. You can also help set the table or wash the dishes.

3 Make a "Give Thanks" box. Decorate a shoe box with pretty wrapping paper. Then give everyone at the dinner table a small piece of paper. Have them write their names and something they are thankful for. Then ask them to put their papers in the box. After dinner, read the pieces of paper out loud for everyone to hear.

4 Have a table runner decorating party. Follow the directions on page 16. Instead of doing it all yourself, let everyone help with the decorating. Ask everyone to write what they are thankful for on the runner.

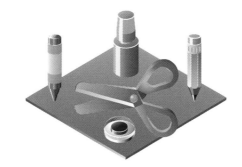